Responsibility

Honesty

Ecology

Friendship

Creativity

Trust

Respect

CLASSIC STORIES FROM
AROUND THE WORLD

A Child's book of Values

PAULIST PRESS
New York / Mahwah, NJ

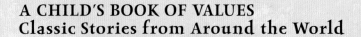

A CHILD'S BOOK OF VALUES
Classic Stories from Around the World

Adaptation of texts: **Esteve Pujol i Pons**
Revision of the adaptation: **Mercè Moreno**
Illustrations, ornamental borders and cover: **Adrià Fruitós**
Design and page makeup: **Leonardo Ribero**

Original Spanish Title: *El Gran Libro de Cuentos con Valores*
First Edition: March 2009

© Copyright ParramonPaidotribo. World Rights
Published by Parramon Paidotribo, S.L., Badalona, Spain

English-language edition
Copyright © 2012 by Paulist Press, Inc.

ISBN 978-0-8091-6765-4

Library of Congress Control Number: 2012934395

Published by
Paulist Press, Inc.
997 Macarthur Boulevard
Mahwah, New Jersey 07430

www.paulistpress.com

Production: **Sagrafic, S.L.**

Printed in China

CLASSIC STORIES FROM
AROUND THE WORLD

A Child's book of Values

Texts: Esteve Pujol i Pons

Illustrations: Adrià Fruitós

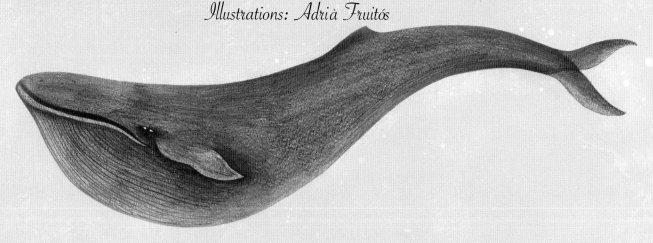

Contents

Introduction

The most effective method of educating in values is seen in the happy testimony of adults. Abundant words may be not just useless, but damaging. We have to mistrust moral sermons: our children already know what we are going to say, what our advice will be.
But we do need to link discreetly, at the appropriate moment, some reflection to our example.

Stories are found halfway between verbal explanations and life itself. They do not place moral lessons in the foreground, but they reflect aspects of human behavior and provide ethical symbols with their characters. Add the interest of the tale, and it becomes easy to remember. Cultures throughout history have understood tales in this way, as we show in this book.

The question is not to moralize in stories, but rather to provide pleasure in the listening and to extract from them a lesson for living.
It is like the behavior of a teacher; although we do not live honestly in order to educate others, our behavior is the best lesson. We do not act to educate; we educate by acting. We do not tell stories to educate; we educate by telling stories.

Spanish Folk Tale

The Wooden Spoon

nce upon a time, there was a family consisting of a couple, their nine-year-old son and the grandfather. They lived together in harmony. The father and mother worked to provide for the family and share the housework. The boy went to school and was a good and resourceful student. When he was not in class, he enjoyed playing with his friends like children do the world over.

His grandfather was now old; he had spent his life working manually from sun-up to sun-down, though tiredness had never halted his efforts to provide his family with food and comfort. But so much labor for so long had a painful consequence: his hands trembled like the leaves of a tree in the autumn wind. Despite his efforts, he often dropped things, which sometimes smashed into pieces when they hit the floor.

At meal times, he would fail to get his spoon to his mouth and food spilled onto the tablecloth. To avoid this, he tried to lift up the plate, but it usually ended up in pieces on the tiles of the dining-room floor. It was the same day after day. He felt bad and apologized when these accidents happened; he wished he was still as strong as he had been. To spare him embarrassment, his daughter, the boy's mother, tried as much as she could not to notice.

"Don't worry, Granddad. This can happen to anyone," she told him while she gently stroked his hands. And she picked up the pieces from the floor as discreetly as she could.

But the father, his son-in-law, did not feel the same. He was highly irritated by the grandfather's trembling. Finally, he made a decision that surprised and upset the rest of the family: he decided that the grandfather would eat apart from the family table and use a wooden plate. That way, he wouldn't stain tablecloths or break crockery.

From then on, the grandfather ate his meals off his wooden plate in a corner of the dining room. He gently shook his head in resignation and sometimes dried the tears that slid down his cheeks. This humiliation was very hard to take. There was a cold and uncomfortable silence at meal times: the peaceful conversations and smiles had disappeared. Several weeks went by. One afternoon, when the son-in-law returned home, he found his son immersed in a mysterious task. The boy was working hard on a piece of wood with a kitchen knife, carefully shaving off bits like a master craftsman. After watching him for a few minutes, the father, full of curiosity, asked him, "What are you doing, son, with so much concentration? Is it a task assigned at school?"

"No, father," replied the boy.

"Perhaps it's a present for your mother?" the father.

"No, it's not a present," the boy replied without raising his eyes.

"Then, what is it? Can't you tell me?"

"Of course I can, Dad. I am making a wooden plate for when you're old and your hands shake."

So it was that the man learnt his lesson. From then on, the old man once again sat at the table with the whole family.

The father understood that if he did not respect the grandfather, his son would not respect him. Do not ask of others what you yourself do not do.

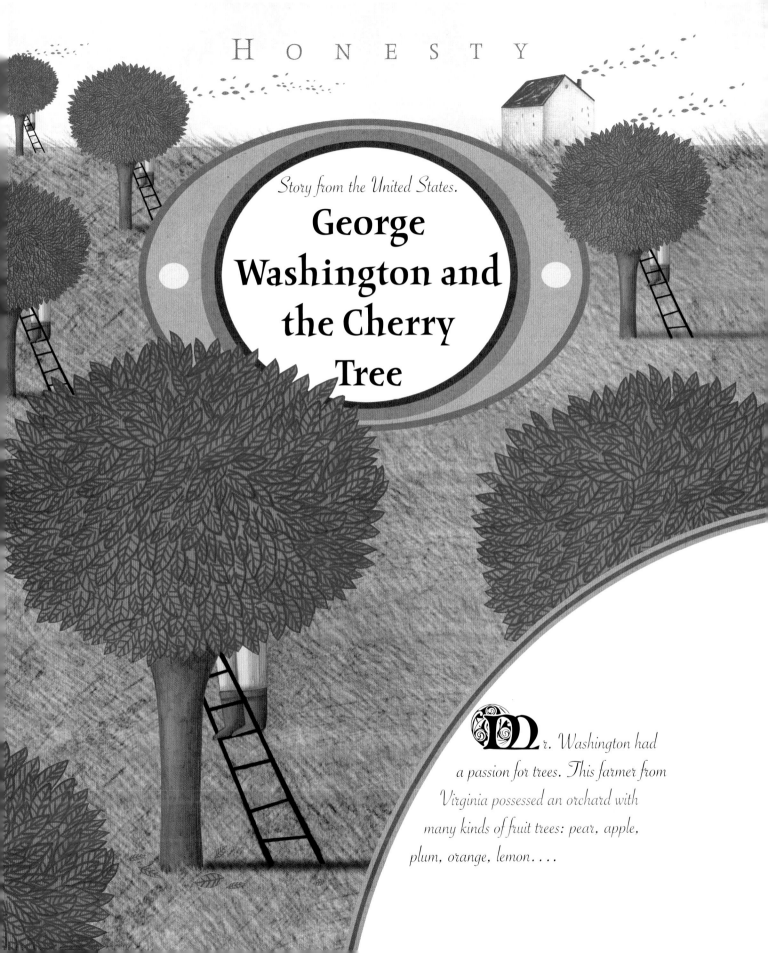

Story from the United States.

George Washington and the Cherry Tree

r. Washington had
a passion for trees. This farmer from
Virginia possessed an orchard with
many kinds of fruit trees: pear, apple,
plum, orange, lemon....

One day he got a cherry tree from Europe. It was not an ordinary cherry tree like his others, but a rare kind. Its shape was unusual and its fruit had undreamt-of transparency and sweetness. Mr. Washington was especially fond of it and had it planted in a corner of the orchard that was well protected from wind and frost. He did not want this tree to suffer any harm. He warned his family members and servants to be especially careful with it.

The following spring, the leaves and tender buds of the tree began to grow and a few pink flowers timidly announced the first fruit. Mr. Washington was proud of his exotic cherry tree.

His young son, George, loved to run through the orchard. It was his playground, where he made great discoveries. Sometimes he even wanted to help the gardeners in their chores.

One day, he found a sharp and shining hatchet among the field tools. That hatchet would allow him to imitate the work of the gardeners that he most admired: cutting off dry branches or pruning dead trunks and extra branches.

The gardeners were still resting after lunch. The midday sun at the end of May encouraged a short doze in the shade. Young George took the hatchet and began to play. With no one watching, he chopped everything he came across. What a misfortune! The cherry tree, his father's delight, received a fatal blow on its still-weak trunk and split in two.

In the afternoon, when a light breeze came up, his father went for his daily evening walk round the orchard. To his shock, he found that his beloved cherry tree was split in half and the leaves and flowers were starting to wilt. He asked everyone who was responsible. No one told him. At last he asked his son. "George," he said, "do you know who killed my cherry tree?"

"Father, I cannot lie to you. I did it with the garden hatchet."

Mr. Washington's gesture of outrage and severe look were the worst punishment George could receive. He went to his room ashamed of what he had done, but above all saddened by the grief he had caused his father.

After a while—which seemed like a century to the boy—his father entered the room. The two looked at each other for a long time without saying a word. Finally, George lowered his eyes in expectation of the reprimand and punishment he was going to receive.

"My son, why did you cut down the cherry tree?"

"I didn't realize what I was doing. I was playing and…."

"And you paid no attention to my warnings."

"Forgive me, Father," George muttered, his cheeks blushing. "Forgive me."

Mr. Washington caressed George's hair while he said, "I am sorry to have lost my cherry

tree, very sorry. However, I am pleased you have been so honest and brave in telling the truth. I prefer your honesty to an entire orchard of cherry trees. Never forget it, my son."

Young George never forgot it. When he was President of the United States, he remembered, repeated, and practiced the lesson he had learned when young.

Young George preferred to be honest rather than lie to his own advantage. Honesty is superior to all wealth.

The Brothers Grimm

The Musicians of Bremen

A peasant had a very hard-working donkey. For years and years, the donkey carried a huge number of sacks of flour to the mill without complaint. But one day his feet no longer held him up and his back said "Enough." The peasant decided to kill the donkey. When the donkey realized what was up, he fled towards the city of Bremen, thinking that there he could work as a musician in the band.

Along the way, he met a hunting dog lying on the ground, panting as if he had run a long way.

"You look worn out, my friend," said the donkey.

"Oh, poor me! I'm old and no use for hunting, and my master wanted to kill me. Luckily, I was able to get away! But how will I earn my keep now?"

"Come with me to Bremen," the donkey said. "We will see if we can find work as musicians. I'll bang the drums and you can play the guitar."

The dog liked the idea and they went on together.

They hadn't walked far when they found a poor, hungry-looking cat.

"Hey, whiskers, what's up?" asked the donkey.

"Well, you see, now I'm old, and my teeth are no longer sharp. I'd rather lie by the fire than chase mice, so the old lady wanted to drown me. I managed to flee, but where will I go now?"

"Come with us. You're a fantastic musician and they're sure to want you in the Bremen band."

The cat liked the idea and joined the donkey and the dog.

Some time later, the three fugitives reached a farm. Standing on the porch, a rooster was crowing with all his might.

"Those shouts are piercing my brain," said the donkey. "What's up, cock?"

"Tomorrow is Sunday. The lady has guests coming and she's told the cook to throw me in the pot. Tonight they want to cut my throat. That's why I'm singing, while I still can."

"Look, red-comb, you'd better come with us. We're going to Bremen and with your fine voice and our band, we'll be rich."

"That's a very good idea," said the rooster.

And so the four went on towards Bremen. But they couldn't make it that day. Night fell and they had to sleep in the forest. The donkey and dog lay down under a tall tree, the cat jumped onto a branch and the rooster climbed to the top of the tree.

Before going to sleep, the rooster looked all round and noticed a little light in the distance. He called out to his companions at once, "Hey, there must be a house not far away.

"I think the best thing we can do is to go and check it out, said the donkey.

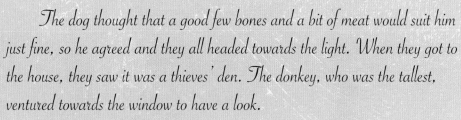

The dog thought that a good few bones and a bit of meat would suit him just fine, so he agreed and they all headed towards the light. When they got to the house, they saw it was a thieves' den. The donkey, who was the tallest, ventured towards the window to have a look.

"What can you see?" the rooster asked.

"What do I see? A table full of food and a band of robbers stuffing themselves."

"Goodness, that would suit me fine," said the rooster.

"Of course!" added the donkey. So the four animals thought about the best way to scare the robbers off.

At last, they found the solution. The donkey put his feet on the window's edge, the dog stood on the donkey's shoulders, the cat climbed onto the dog, and the rooster perched on the cat's head. In this position, when the signal was given, they began to shout all at once. The donkey brayed, the dog barked, the cat mewed, and the rooster crowed. Suddenly they hurled themselves against the window and smashed it to pieces.

The robbers leapt up terrified, and fled into the forest, thinking they had seen a ghost. The four friends sat down at the table and ate what the robbers had left until they were ready to burst.

When they had finished, they put out the light and each of them looked for a bed. The donkey stretched out on the hay, the dog behind the door, the cat by the hearth, and the rooster on a beam. At midnight the robber captain, seeing that the house was dark and quiet, said, "We shouldn't have let ourselves be so frightened." And he ordered one of the robbers to go and have a look.

The robber entered the kitchen planning to stoke up the fire. Thinking that the cat's shining eyes were coals, he stretched out a match to light them. But the cat, in no mood for jokes, screeched and scratched his face.

Frightened, the robber jumped back to the door, but there the dog jumped up and sunk its teeth in his leg. Rushing out, he met the donkey, who kicked him twice while the rooster sang out from the beam: "Cock-a-doodle-do!"

The confused robber raced into the forest and told the captain, "In the house there's a witch who screeches and scratches, and a huge man who stuck a knife in my leg. Outside, a black monster almost knocked me out cold, and in the eaves of the house a guard shouted, "Who goes there?"

On hearing this, the robbers were so scared they never returned.

The house suited the four musicians so well that they never reached Bremen. And let whoever doesn't believe it go and have a look.

The musicians of Bremen are together. They trust each other, help each other, and respect their different tastes. Life without friendship is like a world without sunlight.

Félix María Samaniego

The Wolf and the Dog

Once upon a time, a wolf, more hungry than malicious, was roaming at the edge of a forest. In the distance, he spotted a cottage with a chimney smoking above the reddish roof. The wolf looked at it with flashing eyes. His pricked ears caught the baa-ing of the sheep, the cackling of the barnyard birds, and the proud cock-a-doodle-doo of the king of the hen house. From time to time, the bray of a peaceful ass and the neighing of mares and horses reached him. Soon he saw a glossy, sleek dog, in top condition, coming towards him. Its coat shone, its muzzle was damp, its eyes were kind, its feet strong and tail raised.

The two cautiously drew close, each with very different intent, wondering how they could benefit from each other; but there was no malice in their movements. Perhaps it was the beginning of a useful friendship.

When they were in front of each other, the wolf started the conversation. "Good day, my dog friend. From what I see, you live in this country cottage. It's clear you're exhausted."

"You're right," the dog answered. "I live a pampered life. My masters give me food and look after me. As well as the food they put in my bowl, I also have the pieces of meat left from their table, the juicy marrowbones they leave on their plates, the children's leftovers. I can't complain. The workload is light. If you want, I can share it with you. There's food enough for two; there'll be less waste! Wolves don't usually roam through this area, so my masters won't even realize you are one. You could watch by night and I, by day. Do you accept the deal? We'd both come out winners."

The wolf thought it was an excellent idea. He would have abundant and secure food; he would become as plump as the dog. So he accepted the proposal and they set off towards the house that would give them both shelter.

While they were strolling there, the wolf was surprised to see that the fur on the dog's neck was less shiny than on the rest of its body, as if a rough hand had rubbed it harshly. Surprise and curiosity prompted him to ask, "Good friend, I see the fur on your neck is not as handsome as it is on your back and feet. Has something happened to harm your beauty? Perhaps, when defending the birds in the yard from some pesky fox, you were bitten before giving him what he deserved? Tell me, what does this mark on your neck mean? Perhaps you've caught scabies?"

The dog tried to ignore these questions. But, as the wolf insisted, at last he replied,

"You see, friend wolf, during the day, my owners give me freedom to wander where

I like throughout the estate, which is why I could approach you without the slightest problem. However, when night falls, they tie me up with a collar until the next morning. For many hours, a long chain ties me to the front wall of the house, beside my kennel."

On hearing this confession, the wolf stopped short, stared at the dog, and raising his head proudly, said in a solemn voice, "Friend, I suspect that I was entering into a bad deal with you. Luckily, I've realized in time. I see that all your happiness is that of a slave. You cannot go where you want, since a chain and collar hinder your movements. You do not control your own life. You can neither do nor stop doing what you please.

It is true that I spend days feeling hungry, and I have to sharpen my sense of smell and ingenuity to capture prey and fill my empty stomach. But I am master of my freedom. I go where I want. I have all day and night, to hunt or rest as I please. No one ties me up. I control my own life. I am responsible for the good and bad things that happen to me. With all my heart, I thank you for your hospitality, my dog friend. I prefer freedom to your good fortune. I would find no flavor in food served in a prison, however succulent it was. Thank you," the wolf said.

The dog and wolf then parted and followed their respective destinies.

The wolf preferred a hard, but free life.
The dog wanted an easy but restricted life.
Freedom is a human being's greatest good.

Chinese Folk Tale

The Persevering Fool Moves Mountains

Once upon a time, a peasant family lived in the middle of a valley, crossed by the Guanchan, a river of clean water and plentiful fish. The valley was surrounded by mountains. It was a welcoming place, separated from the rest of the world by high rock walls.

Lin-Chung, the father of the family, was a hard-working man who was tenacious in completing his tasks. His wife, Chung-Lin, felt very happy in the company of Lin-Chung and their four children, three boys and a girl, all strong and handsome.

Lin-Chung had to go to the city to sell fruit and vegetables. He also had to settle some important business in the palace of the Mandarin, who was the governor that acted as Lord, Judge and Chief of Police. Lin-Chung often had to go there to sort out problems.

"Too often!" he complained. The good Lin-Chung had to follow again and again a tortuous path to climb up the mountains and then down into the city. The mountains became a wall of separation, rather than the beautiful crown that embellished the valley.

"If only these high mountains didn't exist...," he repeated time and again. Fed up with so much walking and so much time wasted, he called his family together one September afternoon and said,

"Beloved Chung-Lin, beloved children, you have heard me complain a thousand times. For a long time a daring idea has been on my mind: we should move the mountains."

"Move the mountains, Father? This is impossible. How will we move the mountains?"

"I mean," Lin-Chung explained, "that we should flatten the mountain, open a path. It would be as if we have moved the position of the mountain."

Darkness fell and the family continued to weigh up the reasons for and against Lin-Chung's project. At last, convinced by his words and enthusiasm, his wife and four children agreed to start work. Poles, hoes and mattocks, picks and iron bars, panniers and baskets, shovels and rakes...everything was useful in such a laborious enterprise.

How they sweated with their effort! But the benefits the work would surely bring them would be worth the trouble. The rock resisted with the same tenacity with which the peasants worked. Slowly the path was opened but it seemed that so much effort brought very little reward.

Tun-Lu was a ploughman who lived in the same valley. A simple and sincere man, he observed the labor of Lin-Chung's family. He was amazed to see all of them working day after day with such titanic efforts. Finally, taking advantage of a break when Lin-Chung was resting, Tun-Lu went over and said ironically, "Good neighbor, I know you are an intelligent and thorough man. I know your commitment and strength of will; I also understand your love for your family and that nothing in the world would make you harm them. Precisely because of all this, I am amazed that, at your age and

with your good judgment, you have plunged
into such a task. Don't take offense, good
neighbor, but I feel I have to tell you that you don't
seem intelligent, but foolish and rash to engage in an impossible
task."

Lin-Chung cleaned the sweat off his brow with his handkerchief and
straightened his hat. For a long time he searched in his heart for the best way to answer
Fun-Lu. Finally he sighed, twisted his eyes as if he were looking into a far-away future and
slowly pronounced these wise words, measuring each one, "Fun-Lu, my good neighbor, I am
not offended by what you have just said because I know your affection for me and my family.

I am well aware that I am an old man, and that my strength ebbs away a bit each day. I have begun a task I will not see finished, but I have four children. My sons and daughter will see around them their children, my grandsons and granddaughters. These in turn will multiply until we become a people that will fill the entire Guanchan valley. They will continue to dig into the side of the mountain and will conquer it. That is to say, we will conquer it."

Fun-Lu nodded his head and walked slowly away.

The constancy of Lin-Chung and his entire family will conquer the mountain. Great works require great constancy.

Brothers Grimm

The Elves and the Shoemaker

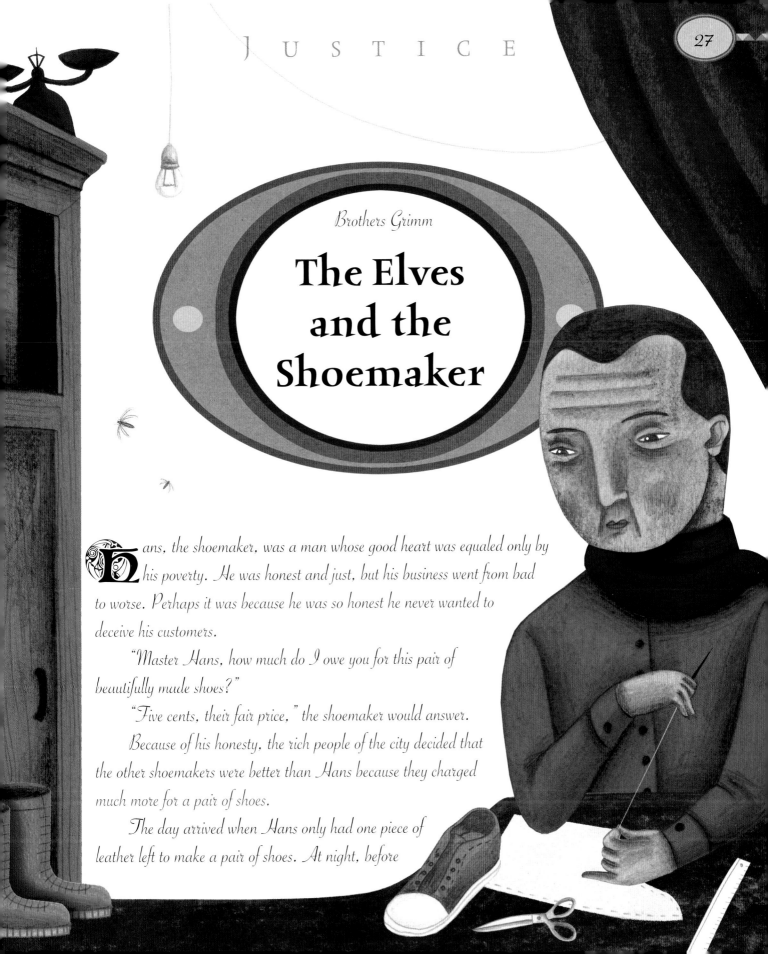

Hans, the shoemaker, was a man whose good heart was equaled only by his poverty. He was honest and just, but his business went from bad to worse. Perhaps it was because he was so honest he never wanted to deceive his customers.

"Master Hans, how much do I owe you for this pair of beautifully made shoes?"

"Five cents, their fair price," the shoemaker would answer.

Because of his honesty, the rich people of the city decided that the other shoemakers were better than Hans because they charged much more for a pair of shoes.

The day arrived when Hans only had one piece of leather left to make a pair of shoes. At night, before

going to bed, he cut it and left a pair of shoes ready for sewing the next morning.

Hans slept like a log all night because his conscience was untroubled. When he got up, he was amazed to see that there was a pair of completed shoes on his workshop table.

He rubbed his eyes to make sure he was not dreaming. No, he wasn't dreaming: they were perfect, a genuine masterpiece.

A customer passing his shop was enchanted by those shoes and bought them. With the money, Hans bought leather for two more pairs.

He cut them out at dusk, but did not have to sew them the next day because he again found them finished with the same delicacy as the first pair. So his business began to prosper. The fame of the shoes that good old Hans sold spread by word of mouth.

Some days before Christmas, when he had already cut out the leather for another pair of shoes, Hans said to Frida, his wife, "Why don't we stay up tonight to see who is helping us?"

Frida thought the idea was excellent. They left a candle lit and hid behind the curtain that separated the workshop from the dining room.

When the bells of midnight chimed on the town-hall clock, they saw two elves, who took the cut leather and with fabulous speed and precision sewed and polished a new pair of shoes. When they had finished the shoes, the elves left them on the table, jumped in the air and disappeared as if by magic.

Hans and Frida were so perplexed they did not recover for a couple of hours. When they calmed down, the woman said to her husband, "Dear Hans, these elves have made us rich. We have to pay them as they deserve. As they go naked, they must be dying of cold in these December days. What do you think if I sew a shirt, jacket, and trousers for each of them?"

"What a wonderful idea! Very good!" Hans said.

And that is what they did. At night, Hans and Frida left the clothes they had made on the workshop table and hid behind the curtain.

When the last of the twelve chimes of the town hall clock rang out, the two elves appeared. They were surprised to see those beautiful clothes instead of the pieces of leather. They were very pleased. They put them on at once and, wild with joy, took each other by the hand and began to sing while they danced:

Our friends, the shoemakers, have sewn us new clothes.

What a shirt! What trousers! How well this jacket fits us!

In these elegant clothes, we will look like important people.

Spellbound, Hans and Frida watched them. They did not dare interrupt the party. They felt happier than the elves.

The elves danced and sang until the first orange rays of the sun touched the glass over the shop door. Then they gave three enormous leaps and disappeared as mysteriously as they had come. They never returned. The shoemakers were rich; the elves were dressed. What more could you want?

Hans and Frida rewarded the hard-working elves. Rather than being generous, we must be just.

Arab Folk Tale

In the Sand and on the Rock

Mahmoud and Ali were so thirsty and tired they saw mirages on the yellow dunes of the Arabian desert. They had been walking for three days. They only had a few hours to sleep because the cold of the night was so intense that they wrapped their colored blankets round them. During the day, the heat overwhelmed them.

"Look, Mahmoud, brother, an oasis of palms with juicy dates and fresh water!" Ali exclaimed, his eyes red with fever.

"No, Ali my brother. It is not an oasis; it is your desire and thirst. There are no palm trees, dates, or water. There is only sand and heat, a lot of heat."

"No, Mahmoud, brother. Allah has laid us a banquet. We only have to go and eat and drink. Let's run, Mahmoud."

"Listen to me, Ali, my brother, don't rush. Allah loves us a lot, but he wants us to walk a good way yet to the nearest city. There we will eat and drink and we will rest in the shadow of the camel-hide awnings."

Ali, obsessed by his hallucination, began to strike Mahmoud, who defended himself as well as he could but his nose was bloody, his skin was full of bruises and eye was swollen. Those were just some of the consequences of the violence that the irritable Ali had unleashed on him.

When he managed to separate himself from Ali, Mahmoud went away a bit and slowly wrote on the sand, "Today my brother Ali has hit me."

That night, they lay down huddled in
their colored blankets. Mahmoud slept little that
night from the pain of the blows. Ali awoke often too,
disturbed by the nightmare of the beating he had given his
brother.

The following morning they walked on.

"Look, Mahmoud, brother, an oasis of palms with juicy dates and fresh water!"
Ali shouted again.

"No, Ali my brother. It is not an oasis; it is your desire and thirst. There are
no palm trees, dates, or water. There is only sand and heat, a lot of heat."

But this time Ali was right and Mahmoud wrong. A splendid lake with a fertile
palm grove that gave comforting shade awaited them where the horizon joined desert
and sky. They ran like lightning. Mahmoud was quicker and plunged into the water
as if he wanted to drink all of it, all. But alas, he had not realized that the lake was
deeper than he thought.

"Help, help me, Ali, brother, I'm drowning!"

Ali arrived panting, broke a branch off a young palm, tied himself to the trunk
with his belt and, stretching out his arms with the branch, managed to get Mahmoud
to cling to it and helped him back to safety on the bank.

Then, they assuaged their thirst with fresh water, sated their hunger with the sweet fruits of the palms, and rested in their shade, so that the heat of the day should not scorch them.

When the sun fell in the west, Mahmoud took a hard, pointed stone, approached a rock beside the lake, and carved on it with deep strokes, "Today my brother Ali has saved me."

"Mahmoud, friend and brother, why did you write on the sand 'Today my brother Ali has struck me' and now on the rock 'Today my brother Ali has saved me' "?

"Because what I wrote on the sand will be wiped away by the wind at once. Maybe by now it has gone. However, what I wrote on the rock nothing or no one will ever be able to wipe away."

That night, Mahmoud and Ali slept placidly, wrapped in their colored blankets.

Mahmoud's heart loved peace; his heart bore no bitterness. You need two to start a quarrel.

Rudyard Kipling

How the Whale Got its Throat

Many years ago, a whale ate tons of fish: monkfish and hake, groupers and turbots, sardines and eels, octopus and squid, tuna fish and swordfish. He was unconcerned by poisonous rays, spiny crabs, or sea snails with stone-like shells. He just opened his enormous mouth and down it went!

Finally, only one little fish named Lively was left in the sea. He was only one, but he was a very smart one. Lively positioned himself close to the whale's right ear, but kept his distance to avoid danger.

Then the whale stood up on his tail and roared, "I'm hungry!"

"Noble and generous whale," Lively answered in a sweet voice. "Have you never tasted a man?"

"No," answered the whale. "What's it like? What does it taste of?"

"It's delicious, though a bit leathery," Lively told him.

"Then you can bring me several," the whale ordered.

"One will be enough for you," Lively clarified. "If you swim eastwards, you will find one of them on a raft, dressed in blue canvas trousers, a pair of suspenders (don't forget the suspenders) and carrying a knife. He's a shipwrecked sailor who, I should warn you, is a man of infinite inventiveness and wisdom."

The whale swam east. He found the raft with the man and, without a moment's thought, opened his enormous mouth and swallowed the sailor with a knife, dressed in blue canvas trousers and suspenders. (Had you forgotten the suspenders?)

When the sailor, a man of great resourcefulness and smarter than a dolphin, found himself in the dark, warm belly of the whale, he began to jump and strike out with his hands and feet, to bite and pull himself about, to shout, cry, crawl, dance, sigh, and strike and move everything within his reach.

The whale got very nervous and asked Lively, "This man is very leathery and he's giving me hiccups, too. What should I do?"

"You should have thought of that earlier!" answered Lively. "But now tell him to come out!"

So the whale said to the sailor, "Hey, come out at once and behave, you're giving me hiccups! Hic!"

"Not on your life," the sailor replied. "I'm not going to do what you want. Take me to the coast where I was born, to the white cliffs where my mother is waiting, and then we'll talk."

And he jumped and danced and shook himself about with still greater force.

"I think you will have to carry him home," Lively advised. "I told you he was a man of great inventiveness and remarkable wisdom."

The whale had no alternative but to swim and swim with the strength of his fins and powerful tail until he reached the white cliffs and approached the shore.

"We've reached your beach," shouted the whale in the middle of an attack of hiccups.

As the whale said the words, the sailor shot out of his mouth. While the whale was swimming at full speed towards the coast, the sailor, a man of great ingenuity and acute intelligence, had used his knife to turn the raft into a barrier. He had fastened it with a very strong knot with his suspenders (now you know why you shouldn't forget them) and had tied the barrier in the whale's

throat. When the sailor, jumped on land, he took the knife with him. He was still wearing the blue canvas trousers. The suspenders, of course, remained inside the whale. He returned to his village, got married, and was very happy.

From that day on, the barrier left by the sailor in the whale's throat kept him from eating anything but very small fish. This is why whales today do not eat men, women, or children. And here ends this tale.

The sailor was a resourceful man and knew how to act at the appropriate time. The greater the risk, the greater the prudence needed.

Jacint Verdaguer

By the Bridge

It is said that beside a river there lived a monastery of holy monks who had their fields and farm on the opposite bank. The river was fast flowing and the bridge to cross it was half-an-hour downstream. If going to the farm was tough, coming back was still tougher, as the uphill stretch was tiring.

The ancient and venerable Abbot never went to the farm, as it tired him too much. Instead, he sent one of the monks, Friar John, who was as good as gold and humble as ashes. Friar John went and returned so quickly that the Abbot wondered at his speed.

One day the Abbot asked Friar John to tell him how he managed to travel so quickly from the monastery to the farm.

"The fact is that God has favored me with the ability to walk on the water," Friar John answered him.

"Why has God granted you such a favor, Friar John?" replied the venerable Abbot in surprise.

"Perhaps because I am very patient and never get annoyed," the monk said in a very low voice.

"Could I pass over the water, too?" asked the Abbot, remembering that he had a hot temper and patience was not his greatest virtue.

"I hope that God will grant you this favor too, if you don't get annoyed from now on," whispered the good monk.

The Abbot also obtained God's favor because from then on he never got irritated or lost his calm.

He went to and from the fields and farm walking over the river waters.

If the Abbot ever showed signs of getting angry, Friar John hastily reminded him, "Father Abbot, don't get irritated. If you do, you will have to cross by the bridge." And the Abbot repressed his anger and recovered his serenity and patience.

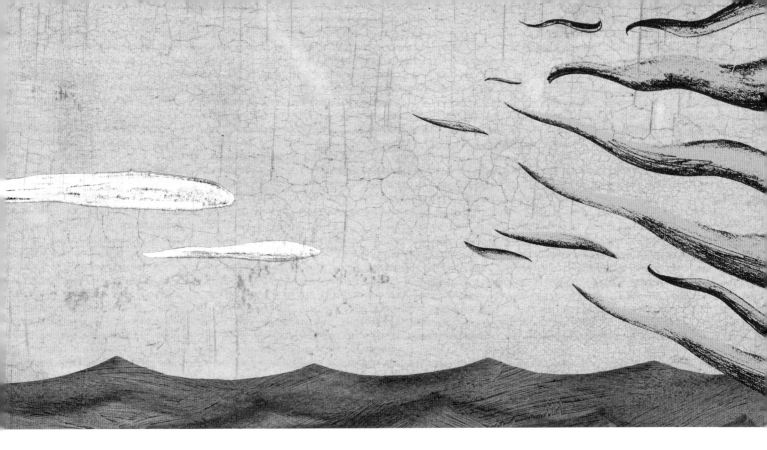

One very hot summer's day, a shout was heard, "Fire on the farm! There's fire on the farm!"

"We have to take the shortcut, Friar John," said the Abbot.

"We will, Father Abbot, but be extra careful not to get angry or we will have to cross by the bridge."

"Don't worry, Friar John, I'll know how to restrain myself."

After helping the farmers to put out the fire, when only scattered cinders remained, the Abbot wanted to know the reason for this disaster.

The farmers were very embarrassed and confessed that their children had set fire to the haystacks while they were playing with lighted torches. The wind had done the rest.

On hearing this, the Abbot's face changed. He looked severe and frightening, and his anger flared up as if a dyke had given way. Friar John tugged at his sleeve and repeated, "Please don't get angry or we will have to cross by the bridge."

The Abbot ignored him. Neither the entreaties of Friar John nor the tugs on his cassock calmed him. His quick temper revived. It had not died, but was only hidden as if asleep.

The Abbot was so furious that he shouted, screamed, kicked the ground, and even threatened the naughty children with his stick.

On the way back to the monastery, the Abbot was already heading for the shortcut, when Friar John ruled it out, saying,

"Reverend Father Abbot, today, as you became angry, the water will not hold you up. We will have to cross by the bridge."

Whenever anger makes us lose a prize or advantage, as frequently occurs, we can remember this tale and say in resignation, "We will have to cross by the bridge."

Friar John was patient and came out on top. The Abbot lost his temper and ended up losing even more. Patience achieves everything.

SINCERITY

Hans Christian Andersen

The Emperor's New Clothes

Many years ago, in a very distant country, lived an Emperor who only thought of wearing new clothes. He changed clothes all the time and had robes for every occasion. The tailors of the city worked day and night about to sew his clothes.

Traders from every corner of the world visited the palace daily to offer their services.

One day, two scoundrels were received by the King after they had spread the rumor that they possessed such extraordinarily fine cloth that it could only be seen by those who were worthy. The cloth was invisible to stupid and incompetent people. The Emperor was amazed at the discovery, as he thought this would unmask the fools in his kingdom and those who were unworthy of occupying important jobs. He wanted to be dressed in the remarkable cloth.

The false tailors asked for gold to purchase thread and looms. They took their time making the cloth. The Emperor grew impatient, since the entire kingdom had heard the news, and everyone was anxious to see the finished garment.

One day the Emperor ordered the Prime Minister, who enjoyed his complete confidence, to see how the sewing of the suit was coming along. The minister saw nothing, but he refrained from saying this to the Emperor lest the latter think he was an incompetent fool and unqualified for his job.

Some days later, the Emperor himself went to the workshop of the weavers and tailors. When they showed him the trousers, the shirt, the coat, and the vest, he saw nothing. He thought, "Maybe I am unworthy of leading the people who have put their trust in me." So he remained silent, but again he paid the tailors.

The day chosen for the first wearing of the marvelous suit of clothing was the anniversary of the Emperor's coronation. So it was that the Emperor, on the eve of the parade and the festival, was made to believe the tailors had been working all night. At dawn, they announced, "Your Majesty, the suit is ready."

When the Emperor entered the workshop, the two crooks were gesticulating and talking non-stop of the virtues of the clothing. "Have you ever seen trousers of such fine and precious cloth as these? And the coat, Majesty, laden with gold and precious stones, but light as a feather? When you are dressed," one of them chipped in, "you will feel as if you were wearing nothing at all."

"Majesty, we will help you dress!" they said together.

They took off the Emperor's clothes and dressed him in the robes that no one could see.

When the Emperor's parade began, the chamberlains, acted as if they bore the train of a long cape, so the people would not suspect the farce. But the people too were fearful and shouted, "What a beautiful suit our Emperor is wearing! It fits him perfectly!"

But suddenly, from the crowd, a child roared with laughter, "Why, he's wearing nothing! He's completely naked! The Emperor is naked! Ha, ha, ha."

The child didn't stop shouting and, like a contagious disease, all the citizens repeated at the top of their voices and without fear the words of the youngster.

The Emperor felt deceived by the two crooks, but did not alter his step or show a flicker on his face. He continued the parade with great dignity while he was thinking of how to punish severely all those who had been taken in by the farce.

Only the child, who had nothing to lose, spoke sincerely. All the rest lied for their own benefit. We cannot live surrounded by lies.

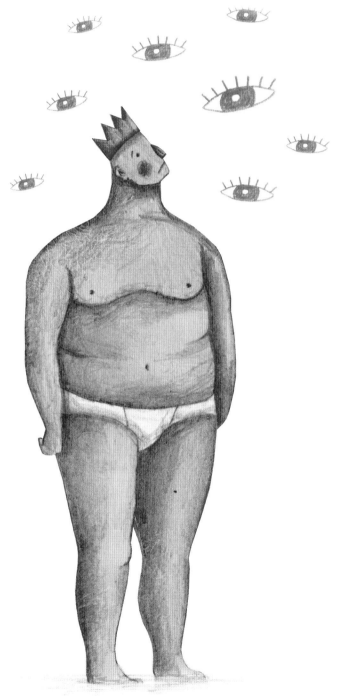

Greek Fable

The Oak and the Reed

In the forests of Greece, some oaks seem to touch the sky with their branches. Their crowns are so enormous that they shelter thousands of birds. They are robust as warriors, capable of resisting the fiercest attacks of the enemy. They are proud, arrogant. They fear nothing. Overly fond of themselves, they survey disdainfully the other trees and bushes that live in their shadow.

"Look at these wretched inhabitants of the reed beds," said an oak to its neighbor one summer evening, mocking the weak canes. "Ridiculous stalks propping up those sad, long leaves. You can only pity them, dry as they are! They're not vigorous like us. Hercules himself envies us."

"You're quite right, strong brother," its companion replied. "There are no trees in the forest as brave as us. We give way before no attack. We stand firm like invincible fighters. Our branches are thick. In addition, our acorns feed many animals that run around us."

And both oaks looked with satisfaction on their enormous trunks, their iron-like branches, their hard and beautifully designed leaves.

Meanwhile, beside the stream that watered that corner of the forest, the canes also maintained a resigned conversation with each other. They were saying, "Who could match the oaks! We're weak. We don't even have branches where the birds can nest. No wood can be extracted from our hollow trunks. We produce no fruits to feed animals of the forest. We are worth very little. Anyone can knock us around at will."

But how easily the wheel of fortune changes what seems most unchanging!

Some dark clouds looked over the mountains that enclosed the landscape to the North. The sky, blue until then, began to be covered by a threatening grey blanket. The wind started to whistle, presaging a storm, like the trumpet that announces that the troops who devastate towns and cities

are close. A dazzling flash of lightning lit up the sky and a thunderclap that seemed to break the granite rocks resounded.

The storm beat down on the mountains and the valley. Hurricane force gusts shook trees and bushes. A tornado raised whirlwinds of branches and leaves. The entire forest was dancing to a crazy rhythm. Sky and earth shook.

The proud oaks resisted, not wanting to cede to the terrible force of the wind. They stayed erect while the storm whirled through their crowns, broke and threw down their branches, and scattered their acorns far, very far away, until they were lost from view.

The reeds were also violently shaken by the storm. They bent double, forwards and backwards. The wind, like an enormous comb, flattened them and then raised them. The reeds allowed themselves to be tossed about as if they were engaged in an impassioned conversation with the wind.

For the entire evening and night, the forest and the wind fought a furious battle. The truce arrived at first light. The dawn brought calm. When the sun crept up in the East, it saw the now-calm forest through the clean, clear air that follows great storms. It saw the enormous oaks torn up

by their roots, scattered in pieces over the sodden ground, like defeated giants. And it spotted the reeds, which were still standing and drying off the drops of water that still shone on their elastic stalks. The oaks had found misfortune in the stiffness of their trunks and their stubborn deafness to the voices of the storm. The reeds, however, had survived thanks to their flexibility. They had entered into dialogue with the wind.

The reeds knew how to talk with the wind.
The oaks wanted to resist it in their deaf pride.
People understand each other by talking.

Russian Folk Tale

Sujman, the Hero

Everything was happiness and celebration in Prince Vladimir's palace, which was undoubtedly the most beautiful palace in the entire city of Kiev. Every evening, nobles and knights met there and, amidst a wild din and glasses of vodka, told with pride their feats of war. The city of Kiev, in the south of the empire of the tsars, was the center of both culture and military courage.

However, there was one noble whose bearing was quiet. He listened to the boasting of the rest, but himself remained silent. His reserved manner was noticed by Vladimir, who asked him in front of the gathering why he didn't want to tell of his heroic deeds as his companions did.

Sujman, for this was his name, replied, "Your Highness, allow me to talk of my future rather than my past."

This reply aroused the curiosity of the prince and all the warriors. Sujman continued, "I intend to hunt a white swan and place it in your arms, Prince Vladimir, without injuring it in

any way. Not one of its feathers will be stained by blood. Not one mark will spoil its immaculate plumage."

"Such a deed is impossible," the prince replied, incredulous, "but I believe you and hope to see this wonder."

Sujman left and spent a week looking for a white swan.

At last he reached the banks of the River Nepra, considered by the inhabitants of Kiev as the father that protected the city and its fields. Thanks to it, harvests were abundant and the country was rich. Its waters were always transparent. Now, however, they were turbulent, full of mud. Tree trunks and pieces of rope bounced about chaotically.

Sujman asked the river why its waters were in such a lamentable state.

"The Tartars, your enemies, are stationed on my other bank and every day build bridges of wood to attack and sack your city. I swell my waters during the night, destroy their works, and drag them downstream. My strength is wearing out and I am afraid I'll not be able to hold up their advance for much longer. Only you, brave Sujman, can halt them," the river replied.

Now Sujman would be able to show Vladimir his courage and patriotism. He crossed the river on his horse as if he were flying over the water, pulled a thick oak up by its roots, and wielding it like a mace, destroyed the Tartar army. No warrior could oppose resistance to Sujman's powerful whirlwind. The wounds he received did not detain his ferocity. When the fight was over, he washed them and bound them with poppy leaves and medicinal herbs.

On the following morning, he met the prince, who asked him about the white swan without a bloodstain. Sujman admitted he had not been able to fulfill his promise, but said he had saved Kiev from destruction. Vladimir, not believing him, insulted him and ordered him to be locked in the dungeon for being disloyal and a liar. However, he sent a servant to check whether Sujman had told the truth. The servant left for the River Nepra. He returned after two days and confirmed that he had seen forty thousand men stretched out on the bank and a huge oak in their midst.

Vladimir released Sujman from prison and promised him every kind of honor and reward. But the noble Sujman answered, "Highness, you did not trust my word. Now it is too late. I cannot continue to live in your palace."

He traveled to the Nepra. He tore off the poppy leaves and medicinal herbs with which he had covered his wounds and died peacefully. His blood turned into the River Sujman, which runs like the Nepra's twin brother.

Vladimir did not trust Sujman. They could no longer live happily in the same place. Let us trust ourselves and everyone else.

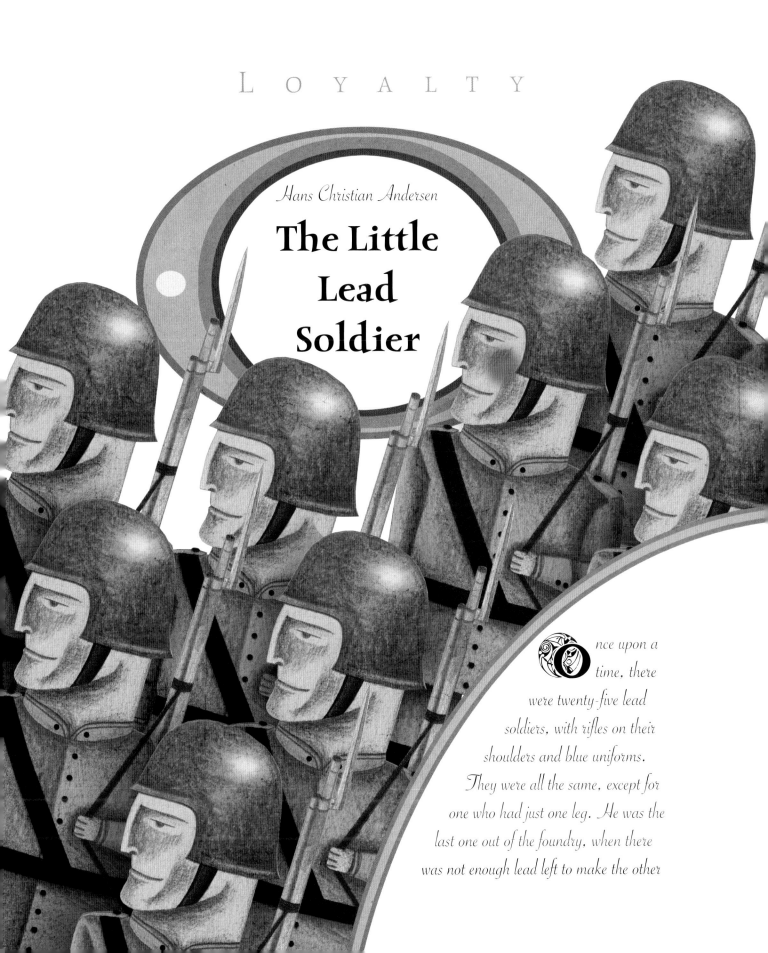

Hans Christian Andersen

The Little Lead Soldier

Once upon a time, there were twenty-five lead soldiers, with rifles on their shoulders and blue uniforms. They were all the same, except for one who had just one leg. He was the last one out of the foundry, when there was not enough lead left to make the other leg. However, he stood at attention as if he had two. This lead regiment was the birthday present of a child, who lined them up on the table in elegant marching orders. The lame soldier was the last in the row.

The child also set out many other toys, among them a magnificent castle before whose door stood a paper ballerina with a golden star on her chest. As she stood on only one leg, since the other was raised, our soldier thought she was lame like him.

"This is just the wife I need," he thought, "but she lives in a palace, whereas my house is just a cardboard box."

At night, when toys come out of their corners, and play and dance unceasingly, the ballerina and the little soldier were the only ones to stay in their places. The latter did not take his eye off the ballerina for a second.

When midnight chimed, they all returned to their resting places and silence again reigned in the wide room.

The next day, when the child of the house got up, he again played with the lead army. He put the lame soldier on the windowsill. Suddenly a gust of wind opened the window and the soldier fell three stories down to the street below. He was upsidedown with his rifle stuck between the cobblestones of the street. The child and his mother went down but did not find him, though they searched for a good while. The little soldier could have shouted "Help!" but he thought it was unworthy of his uniform.

The sky darkened with thick clouds. It began to ruin with such force that the water swept the soldier down the street.

Two boys saw him and said to each other, "A lead soldier. He's lame. As he can't walk, we will make him sail."

With a page from a newspaper, they constructed a paper boat and put the soldier in it. He remained at attention despite the jolts and bumps.

"If only my ballerina was with me, I'd feel less alone," he sighed as he was swept into a dark sewer. There a dark and hairy rat tried to stop him, shrieking,

"Stop him, stop him! He has no passport, don't let him through!" And he chased the soldier for a good while until he gave him up for lost.

Then the soldier heard the horrible noise of a waterfall, as the water from the street cascaded into the river. Among foam and spray, the soldier was hurled down into the flow. The water came up to his neck, and the paper boat was disintegrating. At that very moment, he remembered the beautiful ballerina, whose face he would never look on again.

As he was sinking, an enormous fish swallowed him. The darkness was total but the soldier clung on to his rifle and never lost his composure. After suffering for a long time, light suddenly struck him. A cook had cut open the fish and exclaimed in surprise,

"Look, children, look, this fish has a lead soldier in its belly!" and she placed him on a table.

How strange life is. The little soldier was on the table where he had started out, accompanied by his fellow-soldiers and the other toys; and, of course, by the ballerina lithely standing on one leg. But on seeing it was the lame soldier, the child picked him up and threw him into the fireplace. The little soldier lit up bright red and felt horrific heat, whether from the fire or love he did not know. He gazed on his beloved ballerina until his body began to melt.

Suddenly the door flew open and a burst of wind picked up the ballerina, who flew sylphlike through the air until she dropped into the fireplace beside the faithful little soldier. The ballerina was transformed at once into a bright, luminous flame.

The next day, when the maid raked out the ashes from the fireplace, she found a piece of lead and, sticking to it, a star blackened by the fire but still glittering with a few golden flecks.

She could not separate them however hard she tried.

Whatever happened, the little lead soldier remained faithful to his love for the ballerina. A faithful friend is a treasure.

GENEROSITY

Oscar Wilde

The Happy Prince

High above a city, on a column, stood the statue of the Happy Prince. It was gilded with thin leaves of fine gold, it had two bright sapphires for eyes, and a large red ruby glowed on the sword-hilt. The people of the city said as they passed:

"What a beautiful statue!"

"Who wouldn't be the Happy Prince!"

"He looks like an angel!"

One autumn afternoon, a swallow, in love with a reed that always bowed to greet it, undertook the long voyage to Egypt, the land of the pharaohs and pyramids where the reed lived. When he reached the city, exhausted by the journey and from fighting a headwind, he sought shelter at the feet of the statue of the Happy Prince. "I am in a golden room," he said in a very soft voice.

He had just fallen asleep when he felt a thick drop of water fall on his wings. "It's strange, the sky is full of stars and it's starting to rain. The reed used to like the rain," he thought. Another drop…another…and another. "What's the use of a statue if it can't keep the rain off? I'll shelter under the eaves of the nearest house," he thought. He raised his eyes and saw that the eyes of the Happy Prince were filled with tears.

"Who are you?" he asked.

"I am the Happy Prince."

"Why are you weeping then?"

"When I was alive and had a human heart, I knew no pain. I enjoyed myself, I danced, and life was a never-ending party. The walls of my palace kept out wretchedness and sorrow. Now they have placed me so high that I can see all the ugliness and wretchedness of my city. Even though my heart is made of lead, I cry every night."

"I thought your heart was of gold, too," the swallow said, slightly put out.

"In this narrow and damp alley," the Happy Prince went on, "behind the open window a woman is busily sewing a dress for a noble lady. The poor woman's son is ill and consumed by fever and asks for an orange to quench his thirst. Couldn't you take him the ruby from my sword hilt to buy the fruit? I cannot move my feet from the pedestal."

The swallow insisted he had to continue his journey to Egypt, that the cold was becoming more intense and that he didn't like boys too much because sometimes they threw stones at him and destroyed his nest. But the Happy Prince pleaded and the swallow agreed to stay that night and carry the message. He pulled out the exquisite ruby with his beak. He flew over the cathedral and crossed the river, passing close by the royal palace that spilled out light and music. He reached the poorest quarter of the city. He flew in the open window of the house of the sick boy and left the ruby on the thimble of the seamstress. Before leaving, he fanned the boy's face with his wings to cool him.

"How strange, I don't feel so cold now," the swallow said on returning to the statue of the Happy Prince.

"That is because you have done a good deed. Thank you for your generosity," the Prince replied. In the early morning, when the swallow was asleep, the Happy Prince spoke to him again:

"Swallow, little swallow, on the other side of the city there is a young writer who has to finish a commission by midday and is assailed by cold because he is poor and has no firewood to light the stove. Take a sapphire

from my eyes and carry it to him. The young man will sell it to a jeweler, buy firewood, and finish his play."

After protesting a bit, the swallow carried out the request.

The following afternoon, when he flew to the statue to say good-bye before his trip to Egypt, the sweet voice of the Happy Prince whispered to him.

"Swallow, in the square below there is a poor match-seller. The matches have all fallen in the mud, and she will not be able to sell them. Please, take my other eye and bring it to her so that she does not die of hunger."

The swallow did this too. On returning and before falling asleep at the Prince's feet, he told him of all the remote countries he had visited in his autumn and spring journeys.

"That's truly marvelous," replied the Happy Prince, "but more marvelous than anything is the suffering of men and women. There is no Mystery greater than Misery. Fly over the city, look, and return to tell me what you have seen."

On his return, the swallow told him of all the wealth and luxury he had looked on and all the misery and pain his eyes had seen.

"I am covered with fine gold," the Prince said. "Please take it off, leaf by leaf, and distribute it to the poor, since people think that gold can make them happy."

Leaf by leaf, the swallow obeyed the wish of the Happy Prince. Joy filled the poorest homes of the city. "Now we have bread!" the children shouted in the streets.

The swallow took so many days on this generous task that snow and ice fell on the city. The streets seemed paved with silver. Boys and girls slid on their sleds through the squares and slopes. Shivering with cold, the swallow flew to the feet of the Happy Prince as he did every night. He whispered to him, "Good-bye, dear Prince. Let me kiss your hand."

"I am glad you are going to Egypt at last. I am grateful for the long time you have spent with me and for the happiness you have shared out in the city," the Happy Prince said.

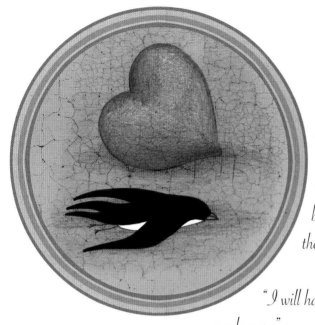

"I am not going to Egypt," said the swallow. "I am now dying at your feet." They kissed and the swallow died with a smile in his eyes.

The next day, when the mayor and his councilors walked past the statue, he saw it was spoiled and blackened, without its precious stones. And what's more, there was a dead swallow on the pedestal.

"It looks like a beggar's statue!" shouted the mayor.

"I will have it knocked down and in its place I'll raise a statue in my honor."

When the smelters were melting down the statue, the overseer exclaimed,

"How strange! There is no way of melting down this lead heart. We will have to throw it in the rubbish." Which is what they did. And there, also in the rubbish, lay a dead swallow.

It was then that God ordered an angel, "Bring me the two most precious things in the city."

The angel brought Him the leaden heart and the dead swallow.

"You have rightly chosen," said God, "for in my garden of paradise this bird will chirp forever, and in my city of gold, the Happy Prince will sing for evermore."

The Happy Prince gave all of himself to make other people happy. It is better to give than receive.

Fable

The Rats' Council

"We cannot continue with this daily torment!" shouted Whiskers, the noisiest rat in the entire neighborhood.

"This wretched cat Micifuz eats one of us every day and, depending on the day, swallows another for dessert and sometimes another as an aperitif. This is intolerable," shouted Delicate Feet angrily, imitating the cat's gestures.

"A moment will come very soon that we won't even be able to leave our lairs to taste a piece of cheese or a chunk of ham," added Pointy-Nose stridently.

The rats were meeting in solemn council to decide what to do before the mortal

danger of the malevolent cat, terrible devourer of rats and mice, baby rats and baby mice.

"I have a wonderful idea," thundered Hairy-Tail, the oldest rat in the entire tribe. "We should work out together an effective way of warning us when Micifuz approaches. This would give us time to flee to safety."

An outburst of applause shook the underground cavern where the assembly of rats was meeting.

"Excellent, excellent! Fantastic, fantastic! Extraordinary, extraordinary!" were the unanimous, constant cries.

"The criminal cat will never again terrorize us. Long Live Hairy-Tail!"

"Now we'll turn the tables on this feline rat-murderer!"

"We'll laugh at Micifuz in front of his own whiskers."

After imposing silence with an energetic gesture of his front legs, Hairy-Tail again took the floor, making a proposal to put a bell on the cat.

Yes! rang out a thousand times in every corner of the cavern, accompanied by deafening applause.

"At last we'll be able to relax with our youngsters."

"We'll sing, dance, go on excursions, organize banquets, sunbathe, fall in love by the light of the moon. We'll really have fun."

At once they set to work. Some went to the corner shop to steal a bell. Others filched ribbon from the drawers of the haberdashery at the top of the street and tied them together to go round Micifuz's neck. The bell was really splendid, bright and sonorous; the ribbon, bright and strong.

When the council met again, Hairy-Tail showed the result of his idea and everyone's work. It was met with extended applause; congratulations and embraces; kisses and whisker touching. At last the rats would be were free of the fierce cat.

"Well," Hairy-Tail said calmly, looking round the crowd. "Who will put the bell on the cat?"

There was a deathly silence. The old rat asked everyone in turn who wanted to tie the bell on the cat.

"My sight's not so good and I might fail," argued one in a cracked voice.

"Sometimes my fingers tremble and I couldn't tie the knot well," another muttered, looking at the ground.

"The truth is, I'm afraid of not running fast enough and Micifuz reaching me with his claws," one at the back said apologetically.

One after another, young and old, fat and thin, gave good reasons why they could not carry out this great task.

Given the difficulty, they separated and returned to their lairs. But they were all agreed on one thing: a bell was the best remedy to stop the cat eating them.

One tiny detail remained: who would put the bell on the cat?

This is the real question: who will put the bell on the cat? It's very easy to talk. It's more important, and sometimes more difficult, to act.

Chinese Folk Tale

Now We'll See What Time Brings Us

Many years ago, in times of the Emperor Tang, in a corner of the valley of the Yang-Tse River, one of the biggest in China, lived a family of peasants. They were honest workers. By their effort and with the help of an irrigation channel that came out of the Yang-Tse, their crops allowed them to live without hardship.

One day Wang-Chu, the son of the family, ran into the house, shouting, "Father, the bay horse has escaped, we've lost it. How will we work the field and carry the vegetables and cereals to the city market? What a misfortune!"

The father, humble but wise and prudent, answered,

"Calm down, son. Why do you call it misfortune? It seems bad news, but we will see what time brings us."

Soon the horse returned, accompanied by a beautiful wild mare. The boy's joy was double: they had recovered their horse and had more help for their work.

"What luck we have had, Father! Now there will be two horses working in the fields and for transport," the youngster exclaimed enthusiastically.

"Why do you call it luck? It does look very good, but we will see what time brings us," his father answered again, looking into the distance.

One morning Wang-Chu mounted the mare for a gallop across the plain, but after only a few steps the animal, unaccustomed to the weight of a rider on its back, reared up and bucked. The boy fell flat on the ground. A piercing pain in his right leg made him fear the worst. He had broken it.

"What bad luck! It will have to be in a cast for a few weeks, and I won't be able to work in the fields. What a terrible misfortune!" groaned Wang-Chu, tearing at his hair.

"Why do you call it bad luck? Why do you think it a great misfortune? Don't despair, son," his father told him. "We'll see what time brings. The gods write straight with crooked lines."

It was just then that the Emperor Tang, a brave and ambitious sovereign, went to war with the neighboring kings in order to seize their lands and so increase his power and wealth. Patrols of soldiers visited cities, towns, and villages to recruit all fit young men and enlist them in the imperial army.

They reached the corner of the valley of the Yang-Tse River and knocked on the door of the Chu family during their midday meal.

They saw that the elderly father's age rendered him unfit for service but said to the son,

"You, lad, get up and come with us. His Majesty needs you to serve with the imperial troops. Pack a bag with your clothes and follow us immediately." Wang Chu showed them his leg in a cast.

"See my leg," he said. "I would not only be useless in the Emperor's army, but I'd be in the way." "I can't walk without crutches. I have to rest for at least a month. I beg you to leave me at home. I will pray to the immortal gods for the success of the Emperor's campaigns."

The soldiers had no option but to leave him in peace. They took some provisions, food and drink, that the Chu family gave them for the road and they left for other villages in the valley.

"Now you've seen what time brings us, my son?" his father said when the soldiers were far away. "Sometimes what's good becomes bad and what's bad, good. You always have to wait until the next day. Then we discover the straight writing of the gods."

Wang-Chu was too quickly discouraged. His father kept his hopes up despite troubles. Only hope keeps us alive.

North American Folk Tale

The Adventure of Ding the Trolley

There was once a little trolley called Ding. They gave him this name because "Ding" was what his bell for warning travelers and alerting pedestrians sounded like. He was so little he was not allowed to circulate through the city streets because of the danger of being run down by the big trucks and coaches. Ding longed to drive on the road, ringing his bell, greeting the children, and carrying all who needed him from one place to another. Ding was very sad. Lack of use made his bell hoarse, his yellow bodywork faded, and his ironwork grew rusty. He looked piteous. The garage overseer decided to sell him for scrap.

The electric dwarves found out about the plan. Do you know who they are? They're the sparks that jump and run along the wires. Sometimes they dance between the wheels and the track, too. They even dare to leap among the tools of the workers repairing the carriages. There are blue, white, and red ones, all of them very bright and quick. At night they met in the garage to help Ding the Trolley.

"We've come to get you going again. We'll jump into the engine and you'll move again. When they come to fetch you for scrap, you'll be gone. We're all sure you can still be very useful. You'll see."

A multitude of electric dwarves got into the engines and started up devices and gears. Others climbed in among the ball bearings of the wheels, cleaned out all the moss, and oiled them; others were responsible for cleaning and polishing the bell until it recovered its silver sound; and others climbed to the end of the trolley pole to clean the wheel contact with the wire. When they left, Ding looked new.

Tiny Ding the Trolley undertook his trip through the city streets. Children greeted him, the young looked out of their windows, older people were amazed, the eyes of the elderly moistened because the trolley brought beautiful memories.

Ding saw a young girl crying inconsolably on the pavement and asked her what the matter was.

"I'm crying because my mother is crying too," the girl sobbed.

"And why is your mother crying?"

"Because my father has lost his job and we have no money to stay in our house."

"Let's go and see them."

They found the girl's mother, father, and little brother

Ding made this proposal, "Fetch your furniture and move into me. From now on I will be your house."

Imagine the family's joy! Ding left the rails and parked in a green meadow beside the house where they lived. The bell rang like the trilling of a

bird in spring. The neighbors helped them move their furniture into the trolley. They painted the walls pink, the windows green, and the trolley pole blue. They fixed flaws, decorated the inside, and planted plants and flowers around it. Soon geraniums, roses, and carnations spilled over the stairs and platforms.

The next morning the trolley overseer came to the meadow and told Ding very sternly,

"You must return to the garage. Since you are useless, we have to sell you for scrap."

"No, Mr. Overseer, I'm not useless now. I am a home for a family that lost their house," Ding replied firmly.

The overseer was not a bad man and, upon seeing the joy of the family and support of the neighbors, he wiped away some tears and promised he would not bother Ding, as the little trolley was providing an excellent service.

The electric dwarves came back and organized a magnificent fireworks show. They also got the radio, heater, oven, iron, and light bulbs working. The electricity company could not understand how all these appliances were working

though the meter dial did not move. It was the electric dwarves' secret. To round off their happiness, the overseer hired the father to work on the trolley.

Everyone together succeeded in saving Ding the Trolley. Union creates strength.

Folk Tale

The Happy Man's Shirt

In a distant kingdom reigned a powerful King, loved by his subjects and respected by the neighboring sovereigns. One day the King felt ill and called the court doctors to cure him. All the eminent doctors met, but they could not figure out what was wrong with him. Days and weeks passed and the King became steadily sadder.

"He has the disease of melancholy," the royal doctors concluded.

They began to dust off old parchments and ancient books on the medical arts to find the remedy for the disease of melancholy. The pharmacies of the kingdom mixed the most unusual concoctions and potions. It was all in vain. The King became more and more distressed and depressed. His sadness penetrated every corner of the palace.

One day a doctor with a long white beard arrived and offered to examine the King and find a remedy to his terrible illness. The King agreed, as did his doctors.

The newcomer examined him, listened to his chest for a long while, asked for all the symptoms and delivered his solemn verdict.

"Your Majesty will only be cured if he wears the shirt of a happy man."

The King's emissaries left immediately down every road to the kingdom's furthest corners. Everyone who at first seemed happy disillusioned them:

"Yes, but my sight is failing...."

"Yes, but my son left home and we don't know where he is...."

"Yes, but this year's harvest...."

"Yes, but sometimes my rheumatism...."

At last they heard a happy song flooding half the valley. They followed the voice and found a man singing at the top of his voice while he prepared a frugal meal under the shade of a bridge.

"Are you completely happy, good man?" they asked him.

"Yes, completely happy," the villager replied.

"Then give us your shirt, for the King needs it to recover his health."

The man burst out laughing, opened his pauper's jacket and the King's emissaries were amazed to see that he wore no shirt.

That man was happy despite not having a shirt. Our happiness does not depend on what we own.

Cameroon Folk Tale

The Elephant's Eye

ong years ago, so many that no one remembers when, an elephant lived with his herd on the vast African savannah, near the River Sanaga in the heart of Cameroon. He was called Baluba.

Those were times when animals still spoke and were much more like us than they are now. Baluba was a scatterbrained elephant. He liked to play and make mischief. He was young and got excited easily, leaping and stumbling about, knocking everything over.

His parents, Daddy and Mommy Elephant, were serene and thoughtful. They often told him to think more and be less impulsive. "With calm," they repeated time and again, "you'll achieve much more than with so much fuss." Baluba did not know what calm and fuss were. He was thoughtless and wild.

The whole herd remembered a time when a butterfly with red and yellow wings, long antennae, and shining eyes perched sweetly on his trunk. Baluba was so frightened that, unaware of the inoffensiveness of the innocent butterfly, he was as bewildered as if a wild beast was attacking him. He shook his ears like mad fans, kicked the air with his thick feet, waved his trunk, bellowed and snorted, until his mother stopped him with some difficulty and made him realize it was just a delicate butterfly.

One afternoon when the heat was burning, Baluba fancied bathing in the fast-flowing waters of the River Sanaga. Before entering the river, he wallowed in the mud on the bank, as elephants usually do. When his skin was smeared with reddish mud, he plunged joyfully into the water, romping like the most playful of little fawns. He dived without caution, as if possessed by a playful devil.

With so much shaking and quaking, one of his eyes popped out and was lost at the bottom of the Sanaga. Now elephants' eyes are tiny, really small. You can imagine Baluba's terror and surprise, his frightened cries. He began to search everywhere, mad with fear. He blew through his trunk, flapped his ears, shook his head, splashed all sides, and above all, he stirred up the mud at the bottom of the river. Every animal that lived on the bank or moved through the water became aware of Baluba's terrible plight.

Silvery fish, green frogs, warty toads, multi-colored birds, monkeys with eyes open as the full moon, fine-legged gazelles, the ever-yawning rhinoceros, even the crocodile that perpetually sleeps, all came to the bank and screamed:

"Baluba, calm down. Don't move like that! Calm down, Baluba! If you move so much, you can't possibly find your eye. You're making the river a mudpool. You'll never get your eye back like that. Please, please, Baluba, calm down!"

Baluba did not hear them. Such was the panic that ruled him that he could not hear his friends' sensible suggestions. The water became more and more turbulent. No longer transparent like a clear morning, it was now dark as a night storm.

"Calm down, Baluba, calm yourself please! Don't move like that! Calm down, Baluba!" they insisted.

Baluba continued to look for his eye. The more he agitated the water, the more turbulent it became and the less he could see with his remaining eye. Finally, tired out and panting, he stopped and heard the shouting of the animals who had come as close as they could. "Calm down, Baluba, calm yourself, please! Don't move like that! Calm down, Baluba!"

Baluba looked at them and shook his mud-filled ears. He not only had not heard them, he hadn't noticed them. He looked at them in surprise as if they'd just appeared there and then.

"Keep still for a while, Baluba, keep still. Calm down! If you calm down, the mud in the water will flow downstream and will soon be clear again: You will be able to see the bed of the Sanaga and find your lost eye. Keep still just for a while, Baluba."

Baluba obeyed them. He stayed still. The waters began to become clearer again. The surface, where the water runs faster, started to look clean, as if huge leaves from a giant tree were carrying the mud far away. Then Baluba began to see the river bottom, first as if a wisp of mist was dancing whimsically through the water, then the whole river was clean, transparent.

What happiness! Where before he was wrecked by nerves, now he went mad with joy. There, on the river bottom, beside some coppery aquatic plants, lay his little eye, like the eyes of all the elephants in Cameroon.

Three fire-red fish collected the eye carefully and pushed it up to the surface. Baluba gently submerged his head and the fish delicately fitted the eye into its empty socket.

All the animals exploded with such cries of joy that they echoed across the savannah and reached the distant mountains. Baluba didn't stop thanking them with gracious movements of his trunk.

When Baluba rejoined his herd, he told everyone the tale of his lost-and-found eye and the adventure of the water and the mud, of the dirty and clean water. After that, Daddy and Mommy Elephant rarely had to tell him to excite himself less and think more.

Baluba had learned his lesson in the River Sanaga, which runs though Cameroon and has clear waters, as clear as a spring dawn after a night of rain.

Baluba had to excite himself less and think more. Reflection makes us see things with greater clarity and depth.

Rudyard Kipling

The Crab that Played with the Sea

In primitive times, the Eldest Magician of all began to prepare everything: first the earth, then the sea, and then he told all the animals to come out. He assigned each one the work he or she had to do. He told the elephant to act like an elephant! The cow like a cow! The tortoise like a tortoise! And so on for all of them. And the elephant acted like an elephant, the cow like a cow, the tortoise like a tortoise, and so on. At nightfall a man with his daughter on his back approached and said to the Eldest Magician,"

"What are all these animals doing?"

The crab accepted the conditions of the Eldest Magician. He became very small and hid among the rocks and seaweed.

When you go to the beach, you will see that all the crab's children hide themselves in tiny caves. They have scissors to hunt food, and for a month they lose their shells and become soft. However, they don't like being pulled out of their holes or carried in buckets to strange houses. They defend themselves with their pincers...and they do it very well!

The crab paid very dearly its lack of responsibility. All must answer for their conduct.

Indian fable

The Blind People and the Elephant

The inhabitants of a village called Tegor, in the easternmost part of India, had never seen elephants. They had only heard about them, and each person imagined them in his or her own way.

A group of blind people lived on the outskirts of the village. Linked by their lack of sight, they helped each other. They had also heard of elephants and on the hot summer nights conversed about this mysterious animal.

"It's a pity there are no elephants in our forests," they said. "Even if there was just one, then we'd know for sure what this marvelous animal is like."

One morning an elephant that had strayed from its herd approached the fields surrounding Tegor. When the news reached the villagers, they hurried to see where this huge animal was wandering.

Knowing the desire of the blind people, the village chiefs had the happy idea of giving them the opportunity of being the first to examine the pachyderm. They would examine it by touch, since they could not by sight. Carefully, and when the elephant was calm and swallowing huge bunches of fresh grass the villagers had brought, the blind approached one by one to touch it. Together, they would have frightened the poor animal.

The first blind person stretched out an arm and bumped into the elephant's enormous belly. Turning to his companions, he said, "Now I know what this amazing animal is like: it is like a hard, firm wall of rock. A powerful, impenetrable wall. An army would crash into it."

Then the second blind person approached. The palm of his hand lit on a leg. He ran his hand down it, turned round warily, and said, "You're wrong, brother. It is like a robust, broad-trunked tree with hairy bark. I have rarely found a tree like this in our forests: it must be very old."

The third blind person, anxious to touch the marvelous beast, was already beside the animal. He caressed a tusk and announced, "But what are you saying, companions? This is the most terrible weapon that has ever existed. I had never imagined so powerful and sharp a spear. Only a giant could hold it. It would pierce any armor; nothing would resist its thrust."

Disconcerted, the fourth blind person wanted to clarify things and rubbed his hands over the elephant's ear. At once he exclaimed, How can such wise people make so many mistakes? It is a majestic fan, which a wealthy rajah would use for relief from the suffocating heat. It is robust and flexible, undulating and fluffy."

The fifth blind person, submerged in a sea of doubt, approached the animal slowly and grabbed its trunk, "How horrible," he shouted in fear. "I've never touched so huge a snake. It's flexible, thick, and enormous. Its mouth blows out burning, foul-smelling breath. It must be one of the biggest snakes in India or perhaps the whole world."

Thoroughly confused, the sixth blind man caught hold of the tail and delivered his verdict with aplomb, "Brothers, it's clearly like a rope for tying up the biggest ships, the wildest horses, or the toughest oxen. Not even the sharpest sword could cut it. It is a rope woven with many strands, judging by its frayed ends."

If the six blind people had not been so wise, perhaps they would have resorted to fisticuffs to defend their opinions.

The holy man of the village of Tegor had to explain that they had each caught part of the reality. They were all right and they needed to unite all the points of view to reach the full image of the elephant.

The sages reached the truth when they put together their different perceptions. Being tolerant means accepting differences with style.

INITIATIVE

Charles Perrault

Puss-in-Boots

A miller left as his legacy to his three children the mill, an ass, and a cat. The oldest kept the mill; the middle one, the ass; and the youngest, Peter, was left with the cat. The lad was miserable with his share, but the extremely clever and imaginative cat told him,

"Don't worry, my friend. Give me a sack, order me some good leather boots and you'll see you've been luckier than you thought."

The cat then went to the forest and made a rabbit trap out of the sack. On catching the first, he ran to the King's palace and said with a ceremonious bow, "Majesty, I bring you a rabbit from the forest, which my lord, the Marquis of Pumpkin, has ordered me to offer you with respect and admiration."

"Tell your master this present has pleased me and I am deeply grateful."

Puss returned to the forest, skillfully caught a brace of beautiful partridges, and went again to offer them to the King. And so it went on for two or three months.

One day he told his master to bathe in the river at a certain place. The King and his daughter were out for a drive, accompanied by the royal guard. When the cat saw they were near the river, he started to shout, "Help! Help! The Marquis of Pumpkin is drowning. Help him!"

The sovereign, hearing the cries and recognizing the cat and the name of the Marquis of Pumpkin, ordered his servants to save the noble lord. When they had pulled him from the water, the cat explained to the King that some thieves had stolen his master's clothes and money, then thrown him in the river. The King immediately ordered his officers to fetch from the palace the most elegant clothes for the Marquis.

The daughter of the King was so beautiful that, on seeing her, Peter fell madly in love.

The monarch asked the supposed Marquis to get into his carriage and accompany them. Meanwhile, the cat approached all the reapers on the land beside the road and ordered them to say that these wheat fields belonged to the Marquis of Pumpkin. When the King asked, they replied as ordered. The King was amazed that the Marquis owned such a big and wealthy estate.

The group came near the castle of the ogre, a famous wizard. The cat, advancing his ingenious plan, went ahead alone, greeted the ogre very respectfully and asked him if he was as powerful as people said and if he could turn himself into anything he wanted. Flattered, the ogre showed the cat he could turn into a lion.

"I'm amazed," the cat said. "But I doubt you could turn into a small animal, like a mouse."

Wounded in his pride, the ogre turned into a mouse and the cat ate him in one mouthful.

The cat then emerged from the door of the castle exactly when the royal retinue was passing. He bowed magnificently and invited the King and his daughter to enter the castle of the Marquis of Pumpkin and eat at the table laid with exquisite delicacies that the ogre had had prepared for his friends.

The King accepted this honor and was impressed by the wealth of the castle and the Marquis's hospitality.

At the end of the banquet, the King addressed Peter, "Dear Marquis, I know my daughter is deeply in love with you. So it depends on you if you wish to become my son-in-law."

Contented, Peter accepted the honor offered him by the monarch and married the princess that very day.

Puss-in-Boots became a great Lord, Court Chamberlain and Prime Minister. From then on, he only chased rats and mice for entertainment.

Puss-in-Boots found original ways
of overcoming every difficulty.
Bold remedies solve grave problems.

Hans Christian Andersen

The Nightingale

As you well know, the Emperor of China is Chinese and all those around him are Chinese too. At the time of this story, the Emperor had the most beautiful palace in the world. Its huge garden was full of delightful flowers, with enchanting colors and exquisite fragrances.

It ran into a magnificent forest of giant trees and wide lakes that reached the sea. A nightingale lived there that could sing such magical melodies as had never before been heard. They were so beautiful that visitors to the garden and forest from all over the world described in their books how the beauty of the nightingale's song was even greater than that of the gardens and palace.

When the Emperor heard this, he ordered his steward to find this bird and bring it to him. This sweet warbler was the most precious jewel in his Empire.

"Your Imperial Majesty must not believe these stories: they are fantasy, even magic," he was told.

"I read it in a book written by the Emperor of Japan and it must be true. I want to hear this nightingale this very night. Whoever finds it will be rewarded by untold wealth. If you do not find it, every single inhabitant of the palace will be severely punished."

Servants, guards, cooks, gardeners, stable boys, everyone went to look for the nightingale.

But a girl who helped in the imperial kitchen was the only person who knew where the nightingale was. She helped them find it and bring it to the Emperor who was seated on his golden throne, in the hall of porcelain and enamelwork, decorated and polished like no other room on earth.

The nightingale sang such a beautiful song that the Emperor wept. The monarch ordered that the bird should live always in the palace, with twelve servants. He could only leave his cage twice a day and once at night.

The fame of this bird spread to the entire city and empire.

One day a mysterious box was delivered to the imperial palace. Inside there was a clockwork nightingale, coated with diamonds, pearls, and rubies. It sang beautiful tunes, moving its head and tail slowly. It amazed the Emperor and all his courtiers. It sang even better than the real one and was also easier to deal with. It could be made to sing as long as was wanted. It could repeat the same song a hundred times without tiring. It neither ate nor slept, nor went out twice a day and once at night. Nor did it need twelve servants or even a cage. Its fame, like that of the real bird, reached the whole world. Travelers came from everywhere to hear it.

One day, when the Emperor wanted to listen again to the real nightingale, no one could find it anywhere. Irritated, the Emperor ordered the nightingale to be exiled from his kingdom forever. He no longer needed it because the clockwork nightingale was better than the flesh and blood one.

But eventually, the insides of the clockwork nightingale emitted a screeching as if all the springs, cables, and little wheels that created the enchanting tunes had broken. Mechanics, watchmakers, blacksmiths, jewelers tried to remedy this misfortune, but their efforts were in vain. The clockwork nightingale never sang again. The inhabitants of the empire were deeply saddened.

The Emperor became so ill that he was at death's door. Weakly, he pleaded to hear the nightingale one last time. The clockwork bird remained dumb and the Emperor was about to depart this world.

Then, at the window of the dying man's room, the nightingale's song was heard, as beautiful as the first time it trilled in the hall of the palace. On hearing it, the Emperor's color improved, his eyes opened, his entire body returned to life.

"Thank you," he said softly. "I expelled you from my palace and empire. Now you have driven out my suffering and my nightmares and thrown death out of my heart. How can I reward you?"

"The first time you heard me sing, you cried with emotion. A minstrel never forgets tears of admiration. You filled my heart. I will sing for you whenever you want. I only ask you not to

destroy the clockwork bird: it has done what it could. As for me, let me go in and out of your palace as I please. On many nights, I will come to sing for you. I will sing for the happy and the suffering. I will fly everywhere. I will visit the house of the poor fisherman and the distressed peasant. I will sing for those at court and far from it. I prefer your tender heart to your crown of precious stones."

The nightingale started a song and flew off through the blue sky of China.

When the servants came to prepare the Emperor's body for burial, they instead found him dressed in his imperial robes with his golden sword in his hands. Most courteously he greeted them, "Good day!"

How difficult it was for the Emperor to soften his hard heart! Sensitive people enjoy life in all its fullness.

Polish Folk Tale

The Clever Girl

Once upon a time, there were two brothers living in the same village. One was rich and the other was a poor peasant whose only wealth was his sixteen-year-old daughter, who was more clever and hard working than anyone.

One day, the poor brother's cow broke into the rich brother's field and ate some of the crop. The rich brother decided to keep the cow until he was compensated for the damage. Unable to pay this debt, the poor brother asked for justice from the Count, his feudal lord who ruled the entire county's inhabitants. Both brothers explained their reasons.

The noble stared at them and said, "Justice will be done, but first each of you must bring me three things: what is most pleasurable, most nourishing, and quickest."

The rich brother thought he would offer honey, which is very pleasurable, butter, which is very nourishing, and his speediest greyhound. That way the cow would remain his.

Moved by this new display of intelligence and love, the Count ordered the procession to return to the palace, where they then lived happy and content for many years, doing good to all those who knocked on their door.

The ingenuity of the girl in overcoming any difficulty saved her and her family. One has to look for new solutions to new problems…as well as to old ones.

Rudyard Kipling

How the Camel Got His Hump

Almost no one knows why the camel has two big humps. Many years ago, when the world was recently made and the animals began to work for men, there was a camel that lived in the middle of the desert because he didn't like work. He spent all day lazing about, biting branches and leaves of the tamarinds and spiky maple trees. When someone spoke to him, he invariably answered, "Humph!"

One Monday morning, the horse, decked out in its riding gear, said, "Why don't you come and trot with us?"

"Humph!" the camel replied. And the horse went to tell the man what had happened.

The next day it was the dog, with a stick between its teeth, who suggested, "Why don't you come and look for things and stand guard with us?"

"Humph!" the camel answered again. And the dog went to tell the man.

The next day, it was the ox, with the yoke on its neck, who said, "Hey, camel, why don't you come and plow with us?"

"Humph!" the camel answered again. And the ox went to tell the man.

At dusk, the man called together the horse, dog, and ox and said to them, "I think it is very bad that in such a new world, this desert animal doesn't want to work. Otherwise, he would have come to see me to be entrusted with a task. I'll leave him in peace, but you will have to work double to make up for his idleness."

The three animals met to discuss the question. The camel heard them and laughed mockingly, "Humph!" And he continued to nibble branches and leaves from the scarce plants in the desert.

Then the genie in charge of all deserts passed by, wrapped in a cloud of dust, like all genies, as they are magical.

"Do you think it's fair that someone is idle in this newborn world and does not want to work like the rest of us?" the animals asked him.

The genie in charge of deserts recognized it was unfair. The horse, dog, and ox added, "It's the long-necked, skinny-legged camel. When we invite him to work, he always answers, 'Humph!' He doesn't want to trot, search, watch, or plough."

"Well, I'm going to humph him," the genie said, going off to meet the camel.

He found him leisurely as ever, examining himself in a puddle as if it were a mirror.

"Hello, long-legged, conceited friend. Is it true what I've heard, that you don't want to work, now that the world is newly made and there is so much to do?"

"Humph!" said the camel disdainfully.

The genie sat down and began to think of a good spell. Meanwhile, the camel went on looking at himself in the puddle, very pleased with his figure.

"The horse, dog, and ox have had to work double since Monday because you are terribly lazy," the genie insisted.

"Humph!" the camel repeated.

"If I were you, I'd say nothing more," the genie warned.

"Humph! Humph!" the camel screamed. Then he saw in terror how his back was humphing once and again, until he had two enormous humps.

"You see?" the genie said. "You've humped yourself because you didn't want to work and were so rude to the other animals."

"But I won't be able to work with these humps," the camel said.

"Of course you can!" the genie replied. "You've lost three days work and from now on you'll be able to work for more than three days without eating, because you will store reserves of food and drink in your humps. Now go with the horse, dog, and ox. Be a good camel and don't humph anyone."

From that day, the camel has carried his humps. He has still not managed to catch up and recover the three days he lost without working when the world was newly made.

The camel paid a high price for his lack of consideration for others. Politeness shows our respect for others.

Argentine Folk Tale

The Tree with the Golden Seeds

In the time of the Quechuas, our grandparents, great-grandparents, and great-great-grandparents revered as gods the stars, the rain, the thunder, and with special tenderness Pachamama, Mother Earth.

Pachamama was very happy to see that the Quechuas worshipped her, not just because they honored her with altars beside the roads, but because they worked the land and respected the trees and forests, the rivers and prairies. Pachamama provided them with abundant crops, mouth-watering fruit, and every kind of animal to eat. The Quechua people were also happy.

But so much food and drink made men and women lazy. Gradually they abandoned their fields and stopped looking after the plants and animals. "We have more than enough of everything. Why should we worry? Let's eat, drink, and be as merry as we can," they told each other with excessive confidence.

And they did what they said. No one thought that the overflowing granaries and barrels were going to empty. The people neither sowed nor planted, reaped nor harvested. Food went to waste because there was too much. The fields filled with weeds. The people cut down trees and bushes for no good reason. They killed animals that lived on the earth or swam in the rivers just for pleasure. The springs became clogged and lakes were used as dumps for rubble and rubbish. Even the air was foggy.

Pachamama was very sad and decided to give the ungrateful Quechua people a scare. The sun dried up springs and rivers; the earth cracked from lack of water; the leaves became yellow and bent like eagles' talons. Flowers and fruit dropped off the branches almost before they appeared. The crowns of the giant jungle trees turned gray. The birds with bright feathers perished of hunger and thirst.

"What do we care when there's still grain in the stores and nectar in the jars? Let the party go on! Let's only stop to sleep!"

One day the people were horrified to find the larder empty. Only four wretched drops of brandy dribbled out of the barrels. Now they heard no bird-song or wild animals howling. There were no fish in the stinking puddles. Only the silence of death was in the land.

The Quechuas had forgotten their duties to Pachamama, and she gave them a good lesson so that they should never again forget her. Wretchedness wiped smiles from children's faces and flooded their eyes with tears. Hunger assailed the adults and the elderly became feeble.

One woman named Urpila ran from her house, mad with sorrow, because her children were starving. At an altar, she begged the goddess, "Pachamama, take pity on my children. They are dying because they have no food or drink. We have been ungrateful to you. We forgot you. Don't punish us any more."

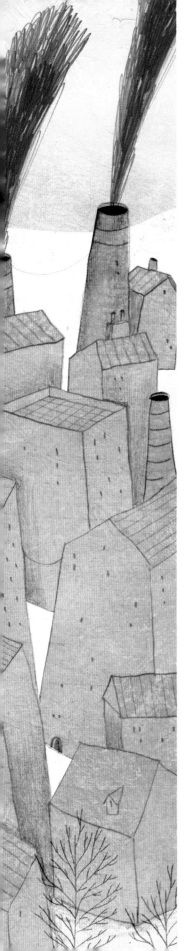

Exhausted and despairing, she slept at the foot of the altar, overcome by tiredness and grief. She dreamed that Pachamama appeared and said,

"Urpila, don't lose hope. You, Quechua people, have realized your mistakes and, upon repenting, will again respect me. When you awake, open your hands and receive the seeds of this tree. They will return happiness to you all."

Urpila woke up and saw that the entire countryside was as sad and parched as before. What a huge disappointment! Was it only a dream? But she remembered that the goddess had mentioned a tree. She raised her eyes and saw that golden seeds were falling abundantly from the nearest tree. She picked up a handful and ran to the village. She told the other villagers her dream and showed them the seeds. Men, women, and children ran to the tree, collected the seeds, and sowed them in the fields and gardens. They even ate some of them. Rain fell heavily and the earth was dressed in green again.

From then on the Quechua people worshipped that sacred tree because it was the love shown them by Pachamama, Mother Earth. It also was the love of the Quechuas for Pachamama.

The Quechua people recovered life when they respected Pachamama, Mother Earth. The world is a legacy that we must transmit safe and sound to our children.

QUOTES ON VALUES

Respect

Don't do to others what you don't want done to you. (various authors)

Honesty

Honesty is respect for everyone and everything.
(popular saying)

Friendship

The greatest loneliness is to have no sincere friend.
(Francis Bacon, English philosopher)

Freedom

Your freedom begins where another's ends.
(popular saying)

Constancy

Victory belongs to the one who shows greatest constancy.
(Napoleon Bonaparte, French Emperor)

Justice

It's easy to be good; what's hard is being just.
(Victor Hugo, French writer)

Peace

True peace is the abundance of goods.
(various authors)

Prudence

Prudence says it is better to lose than lose more. (Portuguese proverb)

Patience

How poor are they who have not patience! What wound did ever heal but by degrees?
(Shakespeare, Othello)

Sincerity

Elegant words are insincere; sincere words are not elegant.
(Lao-Tse, Chinese philosopher)

Dialogue

By talking, people understand each other. (popular saying)

Trust

Trusting yourself is the first secret of success.
(Ralph Waldo Emerson, American philosopher)

Loyalty

Loyalty to others is impossible if you are not faithful to yourself.
(popular saying)

Generosity

Being generous is giving time, space, gestures, words, silences. It is also to forgive; and if we have nothing else to give…we can give money.
(Esteve Pujol i Pons, Spanish teacher and writer)

Commitment

Have you opted to play this part? Do it.
(Seneca, Roman thinker)

Hope

Living always in hope is equivalent to living twice. (popular saying)

Cooperation

With cooperation and concord, small things grow; without it, big things collapse.
(Sallust, Roman historian)

Happiness

Happiness is what moves the hands of the great clock of the world.
(Friedrich Schiller, German writer)

Reflection

Hearing or reading without reflection is a useless occupation. (Confucius, Chinese philosopher)

Responsibility

Consider responsibility as an unavoidable commitment. (popular saying)

Tolerance

Tolerance is respect for diversity through our common humanity. (Boutros Boutros-Ghali, Sixth General Secretary of the United Nations)

Initiative

In urgent matters, initiative is essential or extremely dangerous. Take initiatives with a cool head and heart. (popular saying)

Sensitivity

Don't ever confuse sensitivity with sentimentality. (popular saying)

Creativity

Trying causes no harm, what causes harm is what has not been started.
(medieval aphorism)

Politeness

Eat at home as if you were eating in the king's house!
(Confucius, Chinese philosopher)

Ecology

A thousand machines will never create a flower.
(popular saying)

Fairy tales, fables, parables, examples, stories, epigrams, epic poems, ballads—all have transmitted the science of life from generation to generation since the remotest times. They not only educate the individual but mold the thoughts of a people. They synthesize ethics and politics, philosophy and common sense, family and social values, shrewdness and prudence. On the back of a beautiful tale, rides the wisdom of humanity.

Prudence

Happiness

Cooperation

Generosity

Loyalty

Commitment